THE
STOIC'S
GUIDE
TO LIFE

TIMELESS WISDOM ON
THE ART OF LIVING

RASHA BARRAGE

THE STOIC'S GUIDE TO LIFE

An Hachette UK Company
www.hachette.co.uk

Vie Books, an imprint of Summersdale Publishers
Part of Octopus Publishing Group Limited
Carmelite House
50 Victoria Embankment
LONDON
EC4Y 0DZ
UK

www.summersdale.com

Printed and bound in Poland

ISBN: 978-1-83799-360-4

Substantial discounts on bulk quantities of Summersdale books are available to corporations, professional associations and other organizations. For details contact general enquiries: telephone: +44 (0) 1243 771107 or email: enquiries@summersdale.com.

Neither the author nor the publisher can be held responsible for any injury, loss or claim – be it health, financial or otherwise – arising out of the use, or misuse, of the suggestions made herein. This book is not intended as a substitute for the medical advice of a doctor or physician. If you are experiencing problems with your physical or mental health, it is always best to follow the advice of a medical professional.

Contents

Introduction

What is the meaning of life? It's one of the most profound and timeless questions, spanning centuries, cultures, religions and philosophical movements. It seeks to uncover the purpose, significance and ultimate reason for human existence. Though a definitive answer is yet to be found, there is one philosophical school that flipped the question and asked: *how* do you give your life meaning? How should one live?

The ancient philosophy of Stoicism dates back over 2,300 years and teaches more than just a way of thinking – it's a practical way of living. It holds the keys to a life enriched with wisdom, courage, justice and self-discipline, ultimately aiming for *eudaimonia* – a state of flourishing and well-being.

Stoicism's enduring popularity rests on its ability to transcend time. In a world that constantly shifts, its core principles touch on the everlasting human search for balance, purpose and strength through life's hurdles.

This book brings together some of the greatest Stoic wisdom about how to find joy, manage negative emotions, exercise self-control and cultivate the four Stoic virtues. Through a series of practical tips, wise words and meditations, you will find universal truths about how to think and live well. As Seneca wrote, "Truth lies open for all; it has not yet been monopolized. And there is plenty of it left even for posterity to discover."

A BRIEF
HISTORY
OF
STOICISM

At the heart of Stoicism are its luminaries: Zeno of Citium, the trailblazer who laid the foundation; Epictetus, the former slave who championed inner freedom; Seneca, the contentious advisor to an emperor who faced immense challenges; and Marcus Aurelius, the philosopher-emperor who embodied Stoicism's ideals in the midst of power. In this chapter, we delve into the roots of Stoic philosophy by exploring the lives and insights of these pioneering thinkers. You will see how their profound teachings are not confined to history, but remain relevant for our modern lives, guiding us towards wisdom, inner strength and a meaningful existence.

Before Stoicism

Stoic philosophy emerged in Ancient Greece over 2,300 years ago, during a time of social and political upheaval. Several philosophical traditions paved the way for its development, including Socratic philosophy, which emphasized self-examination, and the teachings of Aristotle's Lyceum, which discussed practical ethics and the pursuit of *eudaimonia*. The practical philosophy of Cynicism, with its emphasis on self-sufficiency and the rejection of material desires, also significantly influenced the development of Stoicism. Diogenes the Cynic believed happiness is achieved by meeting your natural needs, and his simple lifestyle shares similarities with Stoic principles. Stoicism incorporated and developed these diverse influences into a unique system of thought.

What is it then
that will guide man?
One thing alone:
philosophy,
the love of wisdom.

Marcus Aurelius

The seeds of Stoicism

The story of Stoicism begins with a shipwreck at a port near Athens, around 300 BCE. A merchant from Phoenicia (modern day Cyprus) named Zeno of Citium walked the streets utterly distraught, having lost his ship and all its cargo. On that fateful day, Zeno visited a bookseller and started reading Xenophon's *Memorabilia*, a collection of Socrates' teachings. Xenophon was a Greek military leader, philosopher and student of Socrates. *Memorabilia* discussed ethical truths, self-examination and the importance of virtue. Zeno was captivated by the work and asked the bookseller where he could find a man like Socrates. At that moment, the famous Cynic philosopher Crates of Thebes walked by – and the rest is (Stoic) history.

For the next 20 years, Zeno dedicated himself to the study of philosophy and trained with Crates and other Socratic philosophers. During this time, Zeno learned that a person's worth is not defined by prestige or honour, but by their virtue and strength of character. Zeno eventually established his own school of thought, conducting classes at the *Stoa Poikile* (Painted Porch), a public area in Athens. Here, he delved into topics like ethics, the universe's nature and reason's role in a meaningful life. Initially called "Zenonians", his students became known as the "Philosophers of the Porch" or Stoics. Zeno's experience reminds us that adversity can bring a new, more prosperous opportunity. While Stoicism has evolved since Zeno's time, its core principles have stayed the same.

A unique philosophy

Before the emergence of Stoicism, philosophy was mainly enjoyed by the educated elite. In contrast, Stoicism offered practical wisdom that was not confined to a privileged few. It offered distinct ideas to navigate challenges, maintain inner calm and find purpose despite external turmoil. Stoic philosophers often communicated their ideas in a clear and straightforward manner, which helped make the teachings understandable and relatable to a broader audience. It is no accident that the root word for Stoicism comes from the Greek *stoa*, referring to the porch where Zeno gave his lectures; Zeno wanted his theories to be accessible to, and useful for, everyone. Inspired by, but distinct from, the teachings of Socrates and the philosophy of Cynicism, Stoicism carved its unique place in the diverse landscape of ancient philosophies.

Beyond the stoa

The word "stoic" in English suggests a person who can endure pain or hardship without displaying emotion. However, the Stoics, with a capital "S", refers to the remarkable group of philosophers who transformed Zeno's teachings into a profound and vibrant philosophy. Stoicism isn't about suppressing emotions but rather understanding and channelling them effectively. For instance, the former slave Epictetus showed the power of rationality over emotional turmoil by exemplifying personal resilience and promoting acceptance and self-reflection. The Stoic giants harnessed their emotions as tools for virtuous living. Their words and actions pulsate with life, offering a guide on how to master our own feelings and lead a fulfilling existence.

Phases of Stoicism

For over 500 years, Stoic philosophy flourished across Ancient Greece and the Roman Empire. There were three distinct phases, each with their own key thinkers:

- **Early Stoa** (300 BCE) – Zeno's founding, Cleanthes, Chrysippus of Soli, Diogenes of Babylon and Antipater of Tarsus

- **Middle Stoa** (200–100 BCE) – Cicero, Cato the Younger, Panaetius of Rhodes and Posidonius of Apameia

- **Late or Roman Stoa** (100–200 CE) – Seneca the Younger, Gaius Musonius Rufus, Epictetus and Marcus Aurelius

No complete works survive from the first two phases. Throughout these periods, the aim of Stoicism was to transform rather than inform its followers.

Well-being is
realized by
small steps,
but is truly
no small thing.

ZENO OF CITIUM

Philosophy for the hard-working

For many, philosophy seems like a privilege; something you can only study if you're not worried about safety, food or shelter. However, the life of Zeno's successor, Cleanthes, directly challenges this idea.

Cleanthes was a former boxer who worked as a water-carrier by night to fund his daytime philosophical pursuits. As a poor immigrant in Athens, he was ridiculed as a slow learner and nicknamed "the donkey", but his self-determination was clear. Cleanthes wrote over 50 texts and led the Stoic school for an impressive 32 years before his passing at the age of 99. Cleanthes' example shows the lessons of Stoicism can prepare and sustain you in the face of adversity.

The willing
are led by fate,
the reluctant
are dragged.

CLEANTHES

Chrysippus of Soli

Around 230 BCE, Chrysippus became the third head of the Stoic school. Although most of the 700 texts he produced were lost, other philosophers like Seneca revealed his teachings through their notes. Cleanthes, his predecessor, laid the foundation, but Chrysippus shaped much of what is now called Stoicism. He helped Stoicism evolve into a comprehensive philosophical framework made up of three pillars: ethics (guidance on virtuous living); logic (methods for clear thinking); and physics (exploration of the natural world). It is believed Chrysippus died after seeing a donkey eating a basket full of figs and yelling that the donkey needed wine to wash them down – whereupon he supposedly died in a fit of laughter.

Middle Stoa

Stoicism made its way to Rome during the first and second centuries BCE, when it was mainly dominated by two philosophers: Panaetius of Rhodes and his disciple Posidonius.

Panaetius was the last verified head of the Stoic school in Athens and is credited with establishing the so-called "Roman Stoicism". He adapted Stoicism for a Roman audience, making it more practical and accessible. He focused on ethics and moved away from some of the metaphysical aspects of early Stoicism. Panaetius and Posidonius integrated Stoic principles with other philosophical ideas, showing that philosophy can evolve and remain relevant over time.

Things which bestow
upon the soul no greatness
or confidence or freedom
from care are not goods.

Posidonius

Late Stoa

In the Late Stoa period, during the first and second centuries CE, some of the most well-known Stoic philosophers emerged, leaving a lasting impact on Stoicism. Among them was the Roman philosopher Gaius Musonius Rufus. Although none of his written works have survived, his teachings were passed down by his students' notes, including those of Epictetus. Musonius Rufus is celebrated for embodying Stoic principles. His philosophy emphasized the practical application of wisdom for the development of virtuous character, a healthy mind and robust body. As he put it, "Virtue is not simply theoretical knowledge; it is practical application as well."

"The spirit is our queen"

Stoicism's continued influence is partly due to the effort of one man, over two centuries: Lucius Annaeus Seneca, otherwise known as Seneca. Seneca was born in Córdoba, Spain around 4 BCE and educated during a tumultuous time in ancient Rome. His life was plagued by plots, poisonings and power struggles. Banished to Corsica for eight years, he was allowed to return in 49 CE, became a tutor to Emperor Nero and amassed great wealth. In 65 CE, Nero ordered Seneca to commit suicide for allegedly conspiring to kill him.

His early mentor, Attalus, introduced the notion of studying philosophy for practical application. Seneca's curiosity led him to different philosophical schools and ideas; he declared "I don't care about the author if the line is good." Stoicism, introduced by Attalus, became his lifelong companion.

Seneca was not just a philosopher but a pragmatic thinker, who made Stoicism accessible and relevant for everyday life. His *Letters to Lucilius* (quoted throughout the following chapters) guide us through humanity's shared challenges, including failure, grief and death. He urged us to look after our spirit, which he compared to the queen bee in a hive: "If the spirit is sound and healthy our style will be firm and forceful and virile, but if the spirit tumbles all the rest of our personality comes down in ruins with it."

Let us prepare our minds as if we'd come to the very end of life. Let us postpone nothing.

Seneca

Epictetus

Epictetus was born sometime around 55 CE in present-day Turkey. He was initially enslaved, but his owner later allowed to study philosophy, guided by the Roman Stoic Musonius Rufus. Having attained his freedom after 68 CE, Epictetus taught philosophy in Rome for 25 years.

While Epictetus didn't leave a written legacy, his lectures endured through the notes of his devoted student, Arrian. His lessons about resilience, freedom and distinguishing what lies within our control are a product of Epictetus' personal experiences and deep reflections. The fact his real name is lost to us – "Epictetus" means "acquired" – underscores his journey from slavery to philosophical mastery. His insights are commonly regarded as some of the most powerful words in human history.

Freedom is the
only worthy goal
in life. It is won by
disregarding things
that lie beyond
our control.

EPICTETUS

Do what is in your power

Epictetus is famous for his idea of the "dichotomy of control". He believed the most important task in life is to identify what is in your control – your actions, opinions, impulses and desires – and what is not (see page 52): "We must make the best of those things that are in our power, and take the rest as nature gives it." For instance, regret is a waste of time because you cannot change the past.

Epictetus also said that every situation poses two handles; you can grab the disempowering one that makes you a victim, or the forgiving or accepting one that provides an opportunity for growth (see page 76).

There is only one way to happiness and that is to cease worrying about things which are beyond the power of our will.

EPICTETUS

The philosopher king

Between 161 and 180 CE, Marcus Aurelius served as the last great emperor of the Roman Empire. In his collection of personal writings, known as *Meditations*, he bared his soul and offered a raw glimpse into his inner struggles and the Stoic wisdom he cultivated in his youth. His reign was plighted by wars, invasions, famine, floods and a devastating plague that killed millions. Personal health problems, bereavements and frailty added to his troubles. Amid all the turmoil, Marcus found solace and resilience in the Stoic teachings (especially those of Epictetus) and forged his legacy as one of history's greatest leaders.

Training to live

Marcus Aurelius' *Meditations* consist of 400 fragments organized into 12 texts. They offer a window into the emperor's internal musings as he grappled with his responsibilities. What makes them remarkable is their eloquence and unfiltered honesty – they were never intended for public consumption (a fitting example of Epictetus' notion that some things lie within our control, while others do not). The scholar Pierre Hadot believed the power of *Meditations* lies in their unique account of a person "training himself to live". "Marcus is talking to himself," Hadot observed, "but we get the impression that he is talking to each one of us." The following chapters quote some of his most fascinating thoughts.

Dwell on the beauty of life.
Watch the stars, and see
yourself running with them.

Marcus Aurelius

Bringing old ideas to life

Over the centuries, intellectual trends have evolved, with Stoicism facing competition from other philosophical, religious and ideological movements. However, our human need for guidance through life's hardships remains unchanged. Contemporary philosopher Massimo Pigliucci believes the endurance of Stoicism is due to "the basic pragmatism of its doctrines". Technological changes and societal shifts have transformed life over the past two millennia, but the core essence of human nature has remained remarkably constant. We feel the same love, anger and joy, and suffer similar setbacks and grief.

The renewed popularity of Stoicism in the twenty-first century is often attributed to three factors:

- **An unsettled world** – as Pigliucci puts it, "Turbulent times usually bring people to embrace philosophies that are focused on self-improvement and things under your control."

- **Cognitive Behavioural Therapy (CBT)** – applies Stoic techniques to psychotherapy, including the treatment of anxiety and depression.

- **French philosopher, Pierre Hadot** – in the 1990s, he popularized Stoicism as a way to "relearn how to see the world", influencing countless world leaders and public figures.

Stoicism is "both a philosophy of life and a set of techniques", as Pigliucci explains, and living a virtuous life requires you to develop *both* aspects.

THE
VIRTUE
OF
WISDOM

In the world of Stoicism, wisdom shines as the ultimate cornerstone of goodness and the foundation for all other virtues. Imagine it as a special compass that guides you through life's twists and turns. This superpower involves more than just knowing facts; it's like having a magical ability to distinguish what really matters from what's just a passing distraction. With wisdom, you gain an incredible ability to see where your power over things stops and where the uncertain tides of life begin. In this chapter, you'll uncover how to harness this mighty virtue and empower yourself to thrive in the face of life's challenges.

The "chief good"

Among key Stoic thinkers, there was a shared belief that wisdom can guide every aspect of a person's life, with each philosopher offering a unique interpretation:

Zeno of Citium

Zeno said wisdom means aligning yourself with the natural order of the universe; to understand the interconnectedness of all things and live in harmony with nature.

Epictetus

Epictetus taught that wisdom begins by recognizing what is within your control and what is not. He famously said, "It's not what happens to you, but how you react to it that matters." In the pursuit of wisdom, Epictetus advised cultivating a rational and calm mind, using reason to navigate obstacles, and integrating ethical values into your behaviour.

Seneca

Seneca viewed wisdom as the means to lead a virtuous and fulfilling life. He highlighted the importance of self-examination and introspection, declaring "He who is brave is free." Seneca believed wisdom allows you to overcome your fears, passions and desires, leading to inner freedom and tranquillity.

Marcus Aurelius

Marcus Aurelius discussed the impermanence of life and the importance of living in accordance with nature. He wrote, "The happiness of your life depends upon the quality of your thoughts." You are in control of your thoughts and those thoughts lead to your choices, which then lead to the outcomes in your life.

One's destination
is never a place,
but rather a new way
of looking at things.

Henry Miller

Recognize your part in the whole

A central part of Stoicism is the appreciation of the natural beauty and wonder of life. Cultivating inner strength involves recognizing the connections that bind all aspects of life. Acknowledge that humans across time and continents share the same spectrum of emotions, and gaze at the same moon and stars at night. Engage in activities that foster a sense of unity; take daily walks in nature, support community initiatives or environmental conservation. As Marcus Aurelius put it, "Meditate often on the interconnectedness and mutual interdependence of all things in the universe... all things are mutually woven together and therefore have an affinity for each other."

Live according to nature

Stoics emphasize the profound importance of connecting with nature as a cornerstone of wisdom and a path to leading a virtuous and fulfilling life. Living in agreement with nature involves three aspects:

- **Self** – your own human nature, as a rational and social creature.

- **Humanity** – living in harmony with other people.

- **Universe** – recognizing your role in the cosmic order and the fundamental principles that govern the universe.

You can keep this in mind as you venture out every day. Tune in to your rationality when faced with a problem, approach people with kindness and empathy, and surrender to the fact that some things are simply out of your control.

Connect with others through empathy

Recognizing your place in the grand scheme of things shouldn't make you feel insignificant; on the contrary, it can help you navigate life's challenges with insight. *Sympatheia* is a concept in Stoic philosophy that explores how the universe functions as a unified, rational system. It suggests that everything in the cosmos is interconnected and shares a common, divine principle (described as *logos*). This encourages empathy, ethical behaviour and a sense of responsibility towards the well-being of others and the environment. For instance, you can connect with diverse perspectives through open conversations and reading literature from different cultures. Or why not try reducing personal waste by recycling or conserving resources? Personal choices like these help you to acknowledge your interconnectedness with the planet and future generations.

Be a global citizen

Beyond our rationality, the Stoics recognized humanity's innate social nature. They understood that our very survival depends on the existence of others. Living in harmony with nature, according to Stoicism, entails acknowledging and fulfilling our social responsibilities. The Stoics championed the idea that socializing and aiding others benefits not just individuals but all of humanity, as we are all intricately connected. They even coined the term "cosmopolitanism", which means being a "citizen of the world". When encountering people from diverse nations and cultures, it's valuable to remember this concept. Focus on the shared humanity we all possess and strive to treat others with reason and kindness.

A person who doesn't
know what the universe is,
doesn't know where they
are. A person who doesn't
know their purpose in life
doesn't know who they are
or what the universe is.

Marcus Aurelius

Recognize the ripple effects of your choices

For the Stoics, living according to nature does not mean disappearing into the wilderness. Instead, it refers to our shared human capacity for reason, something that they considered to be a profound gift that allows us to make virtuous decisions. Unlike many creatures driven solely by survival and reproduction, we can choose one action over another. Marcus Aurelius said that common reason makes all individuals fellow citizens. In practice, this means that wisdom is not found in self-interest but in being a connected self. Use your capacity for reason to contribute to the common good, both locally and globally. For instance, you can volunteer your time to local community initiatives, advocate for sustainable practices and try to embody Stoic principles in your interactions with others.

Wherever you go,
there you are.

JON KABAT-ZINN

We are not
what we know
but what we are
willing to learn.

MARY CATHERINE BATESON

Make wise choices

According to Stoic philosophy, the opposite of wisdom (*sophia*) is termed *amathia*. *Amathia* can be loosely translated as "not learning", signifying an individual's incapacity or unwillingness to acquire knowledge. The absence of wisdom isn't necessarily a deficit in knowledge; it's a refusal to engage with logical, reasoned arguments. In the words of Seneca, fear and anger can "outleap reason". Succumbing to impulsive emotions contradicts our innate (rational) human nature. Instead, the Stoics encourage decisions to be rooted in cooperation, selflessness and reason, thus facilitating the pursuit of the wisest choices. Before you make a choice, take time to assess the situation, consider the impact on others and reflect on your personal motivations. By being less impulsive, you can prioritize actions that contribute to the greater good.

Look inwards

The Stoics didn't believe in the modern idea of "escaping" through travel. Seneca said "travel won't make a better or saner man of you". Instead, he urged us to look inwards and learn from "writers whose genius is unquestionable". Marcus Aurelius believed peace is found within ourselves; he wrote "nowhere can you find a more peaceful and less busy retreat than in your own soul [...] Treat yourself often to this retreat and be renewed". While travel can be a great way to relax and discover new experiences, the most profound journeys are often found in exploring the depths of your own mind and the wisdom passed down through the ages.

Take time to reflect

Seneca wrote "no one can lead a happy life, or even one that is bearable, without the pursuit of wisdom", which is "strengthened and given deeper roots through daily reflection". Take time every evening to consider all your actions, thoughts and words from the day. Better still, you can clarify your thoughts through journalling, as Marcus Aurelius did in his *Meditations*. Reflect on how you approached situations, reacted to them and the things you did well or could have improved on. Recognizing your shortcomings allows you to learn and make wiser choices, so "the will to good becomes a disposition to good".

Speak wisely

In a world where everyone seems eager to voice their opinions, Stoicism offers a contrasting perspective. According to the Stoics, constant chatter and opinion sharing (like you see today on social media platforms) lacks true value because it's often driven by baseless and biased impressions rather than well-considered thoughts. As Epictetus advised: "Let silence be your general rule; or say only what is necessary and in few words". There is wisdom in thoughtful contemplation and measured speech. For instance, when recounting an experience, try to speak in objective, matter-of-fact terms. By speaking purposefully, you save your mental energy and contribute to a more meaningful conversation with others.

The purpose of life
is not to be happy.
It is to be useful,
to be honourable,
to be compassionate,
to have it make some
difference that you have
lived and lived well.

Ralph Waldo Emerson

Know what you can control

Epictetus said the primary question of your life should be: "Is this up to me?" This doesn't mean indifference or leaving everything to fate; it's about being the maestro of your life's orchestra. Imagine you're the conductor, directing some instruments and letting others play their own tunes. Epictetus' lesson is to recognize your areas of command and those beyond your grasp – this is the essence of self-knowledge. So, when obstacles arise, think: what can *I* do? If I can't do anything, how can I react?

A simple example is encountering traffic on your way to work. You can't clear the cars, but you have another power at your disposal: the ability to transform the moment from one of impatience to inner tranquillity. Instead of getting annoyed, you can listen to an audiobook or podcast, or practise mindfulness. By consciously redirecting your attention and incorporating intentional breathing, you can create a state of inner peace despite the external chaos.

The same applies to the Stoic teachings; if you feel that the philosophy demands too much of you, don't give up! Accept that it's impossible to be a perfect Stoic, but that you *can* incorporate many Stoic principles into your life.

Focus on what you control,
focus on the response
to the things that are
outside of your control.
Do the best you can
in the world within
which you exist.

Ryan Holiday

Premeditatio malorum
(premeditation of evils)

On the ups and downs of life, Marcus Aurelius told himself to: "Accept it without arrogance, and let it go with indifference". A Stoic technique that embodies this is called negative visualization. This involves contemplating potential misfortunes or losses. Ask yourself:

- How would I feel if I lost a possession, situation or loved one?

- Should this change how I live today?

Stoics believed this technique cultivates gratitude, resilience and an awareness of life's impermanence. For instance, if asking the above questions makes you appreciate your loved ones more, perhaps you can make a conscious effort to contact friends you don't see often. By imagining the loss of something, you come to cherish it more and react more calmly if it's ever taken away.

Embrace indifference

Stoicism teaches that our primary focus should be on developing a virtuous character, meaning to cultivate moral excellence and make the right choices. The following circumstances should be approached indifferently because they are irrelevant to your moral character:

- **Preferred indifferents** – health, wealth and reputation. These can enhance our lives and are generally preferred but aren't inherently good or bad.

- **Dispreferred indifferents** – sickness, poverty or a damaged reputation. These can make life more challenging but aren't inherently evil.

To live virtuously, try to accept the outcome of your actions with equanimity, regardless of whether the outcome is preferred or not – it simply is. For instance, if a personal relationship becomes a lasting connection, appreciate it as a preferred indifferent enriching your life. If it doesn't progress as hoped, consider it a dispreferred indifferent, recognizing that your virtue and character remain unchanged.

"Change is Nature's delight"

Marcus Aurelius acknowledged that one certainty in life is change, boldly asserting that "change is Nature's delight". Yet it is often feared and avoided. According to Stoic philosophy, it is a state of mind, rather than circumstance, that creates the problems and difficulties associated with change. As Seneca put it, "We are more often frightened than hurt, and we suffer more in imagination than in reality".

If you experience an unexpected setback, like the breakdown of a relationship, you might dwell on the negative. Instead, remind yourself that change is inevitable. Accept it as part of life's ebb and flow and embrace the opportunity for personal growth. By seeing change as an inherent part of existence, you develop a greater sense of resilience and composure.

Be like water making
its way through cracks.
Do not be assertive,
but adjust to the object,
and you shall find a way
around or through it.

Bruce Lee

Amor fati
(the love of fate)

Amor fati, a central concept in Stoic philosophy, encourages embracing and loving one's fate. Instead of struggling against the inevitable twists of life, Stoics advocate accepting them with open arms. This attitude turns every challenge, adversity and even suffering into an opportunity for growth, strength and wisdom. It invites you to not only make peace with your past but to celebrate it, to cherish your present circumstances and eagerly anticipate the future. When presented with a setback, see it as a chance to redirect your path and seek meaning in the experience. Practise forgiveness, for both yourself and others, so you can move forward with a lighter heart. By learning to "love your fate", you can find contentment and wonder in every moment.

Let fate find us
ready and eager.

SENECA

See beauty in simple things

In 1725, Yongzheng, fourth emperor of China's Qing dynasty, interrupted the affairs of state to take his son out for a picnic to look at the flowers. Admiring life's beauty in this way is part of recognizing your locus of control. Epictetus, whose leg was crippled by his master and who died in poverty, acknowledged that his opinions, desires and aversions were his own. He said, "Man is disturbed not by things, but by the views he takes of them."

Appreciating the things you have is a rational and virtuous response to life's circumstances. Try to actively acknowledge your blessings by keeping a gratitude journal (see page 142–3). Each day, jot down three things you're thankful for. This habit not only reinforces appreciation but also fosters a positive outlook on life.

The trick is to get our values right so that the things we react strongly to are the ones that truly matter for a human being.

Margaret Graver

THE
VIRTUE
OF
COURAGE

Audaces Fortuna Iuvat is a Latin proverb that is almost as old as Stoicism, typically translated as "fortune favours the brave". The ancient Romans were encouraged to act boldly in the face of danger to impress the goddess of luck, Fortuna. Facing challenges and adversity with courage is an idea that also aligns with Stoic philosophy. As this chapter reveals, the Stoics considered courage a vital tool when wisdom is under pressure. Rather than focusing on bravery in the rare event of physical danger, the Stoics viewed courage in everyday life as being persistent, showing compassion and putting others before yourself.

Once we give ourselves
permission to open up
and play with lots of
potential ideas and
possibilities, creativity
rewards us, enabling us
to spot opportunities
in unlikely places.

Tara Swart

Choose to be challenged

The Stoics believed that true wisdom and virtue are cultivated through facing and overcoming life's trials and tribulations. Rather than avoiding or fearing challenges, they embraced them, knowing that they provide opportunities for personal growth and the development of inner strength. Marcus Aurelius, a Roman, wrote his innermost thoughts in his non-native language, Greek (his first language was Latin); even in his private writings he deliberately challenged himself. To actively engage with situations that may test your character and virtue, seek out new challenges, such as learning a new skill or running a marathon.

The more you
schedule and
practise discomfort
deliberately, the less
unplanned discomfort
will throw off your life
and control your life.

TIM FERRISS

Train your resilience

Several of the ancient Stoics were known for sleeping on the floor, dressing in shabby clothing, fasting and exposing themselves to extreme temperatures. They believed that developing resilience improved their ability to deal with the chaos of life. One simple way to expand your comfort zone is by regularly exposing yourself to situations you would normally avoid for fear of embarrassment. For instance, try walking barefoot outside, asking for a pay rise or wearing your most outrageous clothes! By training yourself to be resilient in the face of ridicule, you will only feel shame when it's truly deserved.

Prepare for bad luck

To be successful in anything, you have to be ready to fail. If you aspire to start your own business, be prepared to encounter setbacks; consider saving an emergency fund or learning additional skills. Being prepared for failure by having a back-up plan – perhaps a part-time job or freelancing gigs – gives you the courage to try to succeed; if you can't endure disappointment, you're more likely to avoid the risk. As Marcus Aurelius put it: "Get busy with life's purpose, toss aside empty hopes, get active in your own rescue – if you care for yourself at all – and do it while you can."

It is better to live your own destiny imperfectly than to live an imitation of somebody else's life with perfection.

The *Bhagavad Gita*

Persist and resist

Epictetus said that two words are necessary to "lead a mainly blameless and untroubled life: persist and resist".

Persist

Epictetus taught that true courage is the ability to endure difficulties and maintain one's commitment to virtue, even when faced with external obstacles. Seneca likewise argued that a brave person is not someone who lacks fear or desire, but the person who experiences these feelings and strives to overcome them. So when you are faced with challenges and adversity, try to avoid the temptation of giving in to fears or acting unvirtuously; persist in the face of the obstacle.

Resist

Stoicism encourages you to practise resisting external influences that could lead to vice or moral weakness. It's the idea of refusing the pull of desires, emotions or societal pressures that can detract you from doing the right thing.

You will inevitably experience discomfort, fear and desire throughout your life – the aim is to endure painful feelings and rise above them by reminding yourself of your principles and the importance of doing what is morally right, even in the face of external expectations.

... there was something comforting and liberating about being an actual definite someone, rather than a collection of contradictory potential someones.

Jonathan Franzen

Practise adversity

Disappointments and failures are universal experiences that often happen when we least expect them. Trying to avoid them can make us anxious and insecure. The Stoics therefore urged us to practise adversity. For instance, if you fear losing wealth, Seneca advised: "Set aside a certain number of days, during which you shall be content with the scantiest and cheapest fare, with coarse and rough dress, saying to yourself the while: 'Is this the condition that I feared?'" Perhaps you could walk to distant locations to put your body to the test, try living without certain luxuries for a few days, or set yourself a strict budget for a period of time. Training yourself in a controlled environment better prepares you for any future struggles.

See obstacles
as opportunities

The Stoics viewed challenges in life as opportunities for personal growth; they propel our lives forward and help us to achieve our goals. Marcus Aurelius wrote: "The impediment to action advances action. What stands in the way becomes the way."

When a problem arises in your life, Stoicism urges you to avoid freezing in the face of uncertainty or dwelling on the negative; instead, make courage your choice.

Think about the skills and qualities you need to resolve any issues that arise. Put simply: don't focus on the problem itself, focus on what it *asks* of you. Do you need to be decisive or empathetic? Does courage require you to be humble, or imaginative?

Obstacles in life often help to reveal solutions and alternative approaches that you might otherwise have overlooked. Seneca wrote, "Let philosophy scrape off your own faults, rather than be a way to rail against the faults of others." Dwelling on other people's faults multiplies your own, and focusing on negatives only stalls you. Instead, identify the strengths you have and the solutions available to overcome the problem, and take action to navigate the obstacle.

We might not be emperors,
but the world is still
constantly testing us.
It asks: Are you worthy?
Can you get past the
things that inevitably
fall in your way? Will
you stand up and show
us what you're made of?

Ryan Holiday

Stay true to your principles

In the realm of Stoic courage, staying true to your principles is an active, unyielding act. If you ever find yourself in a situation that requires you to stand up for yourself or others, or when you can contribute to a cause that is close to your heart, recognize the opportunity to be courageous. Express your feelings with empathy and resist peer pressure. This is the heart of Stoic valour: the determination to confront situations that contradict your principles. It's about summoning the courage to speak up, even when it involves social risks, and pushing for what you believe is right. As Marcus Aurelius said: "Fight to be the person philosophy wants you to be."

All of us retain the capacity to change, even to change in fundamental ways, as long as we live.

KAREN HORNEY

Small acts of courage

Courage is not always about big heroic acts. For the Stoics, it is possible to act bravely through the small choices you make every day. For instance, it's heroic to speak out against an unfair office policy or to challenge a friend's hurtful comment, all while maintaining a calm attitude. Your courage especially shines in self-discipline, like choosing to resist that enticing slice of cake when adhering to a healthy diet, or persisting with your exercise routine even when you're tempted to skip it. Reading this book is a daring act in itself; it takes bravery to question your present character, to strive to change and improve yourself.

Persevere through pain

Struggle comes in many forms, and adopting a courageous mindset can help sustain you through the pain until it is resolved. For instance:

- **Physical pain** – be steadfast during workouts (but not to the point of injury), knowing the temporary discomfort will lead to greater strength and health.

- **Emotional pain** – address relationship conflicts head-on, seeking understanding and resolution instead of avoiding issues or responding impulsively with anger.

- **Intellectual pain** – tackle complex problems and new challenges rather than shying away or seeking distractions.

As Seneca said, "It does not matter what you bear, but how you bear it."

What we get out of life is not determined by the good feelings we desire, but by what *bad* feelings we're willing and able to sustain to get us to those good feelings.

Mark Manson

Be authentic

Epictetus said, "If you have assumed a character beyond your strength, you have both played a poor figure in that, and neglected one that is within your powers." Recognizing your strengths and limitations takes courage and requires you to be authentic with others. In a world that often encourages conformity, it takes courage to stay true to your genuine abilities and not pretend to be something you are not. For instance, in social interactions, admit when you lack knowledge about a subject, or if you're searching for employment, acknowledge your strengths and look for roles that match your abilities and remember not to undervalue yourself.

There's no greater
waste of time than
justifying your
actions to people
who have a life
you don't want.

ALEX HORMOZI

Be vulnerable

Vulnerability and courage are intertwined. Acknowledging your fears and insecurities, or taking responsibility for your faults, means opening yourself to potential judgement or criticism. Being vulnerable may not be comfortable but it's a strength and a way to practise courage. Vulnerability is also about staying true to your values (through your words or actions), even if it might leave you isolated. For instance, if your colleagues eat lunch at their desk every day but you prioritize physical health, dare to go for walks instead.

Don't be afraid to admit when you don't know something, seek help when it's needed and share your feelings and experiences honestly.

Vulnerability is
not weakness. It's
the most accurate
measurement
of courage.

BRENÉ BROWN

Admit your mistakes

Truth is fundamental to Stoic philosophy, and one aspect of this is acknowledging when you're wrong. In his quest for truth, Marcus Aurelius wrote: "If anyone can refute me – show me I'm making a mistake or looking at things from the wrong perspective – I'll gladly change." Rather than hiding behind pride, having a fixed mindset or feeling shame in your errors, acknowledge to yourself and others when you make a mistake. Changing your opinion is not a sign of weakness or unreliability; it shows humility and a willingness to improve.

If you can see your path
laid out in front of you
step by step, you know
it's not your path.
Your own path you make
with every step you take.
That's why it's your path.

Joseph Campbell

Act selflessly

In 2020, amid an anti-racism protest that escalated into violence, a Black man named Patrick Hutchinson hoisted a white, injured counter-protester over his shoulder and took him to safety. Hutchinson and his friends saved the man's life. This heroic rescue reverberated across the globe as a powerful symbol of human unity. It embodies the Stoic perspective on kindness as an act of courage. Bravery, in Stoic terms, means acting virtuously and justly, even in the face of adversity. Recognize selfless action as a strength, *especially* when it contradicts your immediate desires, fears or societal pressures and overcomes the urge to retaliate.

When death finds you,
may it find you alive.

African proverb

Memento mori

When Marcus Aurelius lay dying at the age of 58, he turned to his guard and said: "Go to the rising sun; I am already setting." His final words are commonly interpreted as a peaceful acceptance of his own mortality and the inevitable end of his life.

The Stoics viewed death as a way of giving back to nature something that was temporarily loaned to us. Marcus, like other Stoics, was prepared to meet his death because he had spent his life overcoming his fear of it – a fear we all share that is ultimately irrational.

Old and young alike should have death
before their eyes; we are not summoned
in order of birth registration.

———

Seneca

The Latin phrase "*Memento mori*", which
translates to "remember that you must die",
isn't meant to cast a shadow over your life. It is
a reminder to seize the moment and live every
day to the fullest, knowing that time is both
limited and unpredictable. When you regularly
contemplate your own death and the mortality
of those around you, you infuse your existence
with a newfound intensity and appreciation for
the present.

THE
VIRTUE
OF
TEMPERANCE

Courage is a cornerstone of Stoic philosophy, but it can easily descend into reckless or impulsive behaviour. In order for courage to be channelled wisely, it needs temperance or moderation. You can think of temperance as courage's guiding hand, ensuring your brave actions follow a deliberate, rational path. In Stoic teachings, temperance is often referred to as "self-control", and this chapter reveals how it can steer you through life's complexities and ensure your choices are wise and purposeful. Whether you're facing adversity, savouring life's pleasures or mastering your desires, you'll see how temperance can align your actions with the virtuous principles of Stoicism.

Find your imbalance

Temperance is not about abstinence or giving up the things you love. It's about achieving the right balance in your life so its struggles and pleasures are neither completely absent nor experienced in excess. As Seneca wrote, "Pleasures, when they go beyond a certain limit, are but punishments."

The first step to achieving balance is to recognize imbalances in your life. For instance, are you spending many more hours a day sitting rather than walking? Are you prioritizing work over time with family or friends? Find what is excessive in your life and try to counterbalance it.

Only the disciplined
ones in life are free.
If you are undisciplined,
you are a slave to your
moods and your passions.

Eliud Kipchoge

Wisdom in decision-making

Stoicism calls for thoughtful, rational and virtue-driven choices, all while maintaining emotional balance and detachment from external outcomes. Decisions should be based on what is genuinely beneficial in the long run, rather than giving in to instant pleasures or feelings. As Massimo Pigliucci says, "A wise person is the one that takes the right course of action, not just instrumentally, but morally."

To make conscious decisions that are rooted in wisdom rather than impulsive reactions, you can try the following:

- Pause and assess situations objectively, to allow for more measured and reasoned responses.

- Set goals based on the Stoic virtues rather than external factors like wealth, health or reputation (which are "preferred indifferents") and align your decisions with these virtues.

- Practise delayed gratification by resisting the temptation of immediate pleasures; consider the long-term consequences and benefits of your choices.

- *Eulabeia* is a form of mindfulness encouraged by the Stoics. It means "caution" or "discretion" and is understood as a kind of healthy self-consciousness. You can adopt this mindset by allocating time for daily reflection to evaluate decisions and their moral implications. This can help to prevent you from making decisions based on irrational fears or desires.

Make small adjustments

The Stoics champion inner strength over material wealth. Seneca wrote that every day you should "acquire something which will help you to face poverty, or death, and other ills as well".

Instead of reacting impulsively on a day-by-day basis, you can cultivate long-term resilience and wisdom by considering these key adjustments:

- **Physical fitness** – prioritize cardio, nutrition, resistance training and flexibility.

- **Mental fitness** – read widely, maintain a healthy diet and sleep routine, and care for your mental well-being.

- **Emotional fitness** – nurture emotional fitness through practices such as mindfulness, self-reflection and building healthy emotional coping mechanisms.

Embracing these practices fortifies your inner resources to confront life's obstacles.

Talent is insignificant.
I know a lot of
talented ruins. Beyond
talent lie all the usual
words: discipline,
love, luck, but most
of all, endurance.

JAMES BALDWIN

Reject materialism

Seneca was one of the richest men in Ancient Rome. He acquired vast amounts of wealth and property while serving as advisor to the Emperor Nero. It is perhaps for this reason that he questioned wealth and explored how it damaged the owner. For Seneca, wealth diminished the peace of mind needed for virtuous living. He wrote, "It is not the man who has too little who is poor, but the one who hankers after more."

Stoicism teaches that there is nothing wrong with wealth in itself; the problem lies in being *attached* to your material possessions and consuming without any rational reason. Abundance comes from having what is essential. To develop this attitude and avoid impulsive buying, try the following:

- Buy items that add value to your life and align with your needs.

- When buying a new item of clothing, donate something you already own.

- Declutter your living space so you become comfortable with less.

- Regularly reflect on the non-material aspects of life that you are grateful for, like relationships, health and personal growth.

- Prioritize experiences, such as travel, learning a new skill or spending quality time with loved ones.

Work hard in silence,
let your success
be the noise.

FRANK OCEAN

Live intentionally

In the 1960s, French philosopher René Girard claimed that our desires are not our own. His "mimetic desire" theory argued that we imitate other people's desires, especially those we admire. To distinguish genuine desires, the Stoics suggested being detached and deliberate:

- Distrust immediate desires and create distance from them, for instance by waiting a week and evaluating your desires critically before buying something. This also encourages gratitude.

- Distinguish which actions develop your moral excellence, wisdom and the pursuit of virtue.

This way, you heed Seneca's warning: "You act like mortals in all that you fear, and like immortals in all that you desire."

Reflect on impulses

The Stoics believed that if you constantly seek pleasure and avoid pain or discomfort, then you become a slave to your passions. To live a virtuous and eudemonic life, avoid impulsive and uncontrolled behaviour. Instead, strive for deliberate and rational control of your desires and emotions, particularly in situations where giving in to immediate pleasure would be against your long-term well-being or virtuous principles.

When you notice impulsive desires or actions, take a moment to reflect on them. For instance, is scrolling through social media late at night impacting your sleep? Consider the potential consequences of acting on your impulses and whether they align with your long-term well-being and moral values.

I cannot and will not
cut my conscience
to fit this year's fashions.

Lillian Hellman

Rest as needed

The Stoics believed people should not strive for constant busyness or for idleness. Seneca wrote that "the active man should be able to take things easily, while the man who is inclined towards repose should be capable of action. Ask nature: she will tell you that she made both day and night."

Just as day and night each serve a unique purpose, human beings should work or rest as needed. To achieve work-life balance, try to engage in purposeful action or embrace rest as circumstances dictate. Establish clear boundaries for work and personal time, and try to set achievable goals. By listening to your body and making time for things you enjoy, you can navigate the demands of life more effectively.

If it matters to you,
make the time.

Arnold Schwarzenegger

Seize the sunrise

Marcus Aurelius wrote that "Whenever you have trouble getting up in the morning, remind yourself that you've been made by nature for the purpose of working with others." He felt the universal temptation to stay warm in bed but believed in the importance of aligning our morning routines with the natural world. Just as many other creatures on Earth wake with the sunrise, he encouraged himself to rise with the dawn and "go to work – as a human being". Getting out of bed to make a start on your day – even when you don't want to – means you are living your life as nature intended. Embracing morning rituals, like watching the sunrise, can provide opportunities for mindfulness, grounding you in the present and fostering a sense of well-being throughout the day.

Live the full
life of the mind,
exhilarated by new
ideas, intoxicated
by the romance
of the unusual.

ERNEST HEMINGWAY

Manage your anger

*The nearer a man
comes to a calm mind,
the closer he is to strength.*

Marcus Aurelius

The Stoics viewed anger as an irrational and destructive emotion that can disrupt one's inner tranquillity and virtuous living. Strategies you can adopt for a calmer mind include:

- Managing your expectations of other people and recognizing that you can only control your own actions and reactions. The Stoics recognized that foolish behaviour is common in human beings and that acting surprised in reaction to it is irrational. Accept that people are imperfect and that you can't control them.

- Focusing on the harmful consequences of anger, especially the damage it does to your moral character. Actions taken in anger are usually regretted later. As Seneca said: "Anger always outlasts hurt." This can inspire you to change your response.

- Pausing for ten seconds to gather your thoughts before you respond. Speaking to yourself in the third person can reduce your reactivity.

- Being aware of people's different motives and their whole character rather than focusing on their worst trait.

You cannot prevent
the birds of sorrow
from flying over
your head, but you
can prevent them
from building nests
in your hair.

CHINESE PROVERB

Live in the present

The Stoics recognized that many of our worries and anxieties stem from either dwelling on the past or fearing the future. Instead, they encouraged us to focus on the present to free ourselves from these concerns, which are outside of our control. One way is to practise mindfulness, which you can do by:

- Focusing on one thing at a time (do not try to multitask)

- Putting your phone away in the presence of others

- Meditating

- Practising grounding exercises to engage your senses, such as identifying five things you can see, four things you can hear, three things you can touch, two things you can smell and one thing you can taste.

Develop mindfulness techniques to stay present and make more deliberate decisions.

Develop self-discipline

Nassim Nicholas Taleb aptly defines Stoicism as "the domestication of emotions, not their elimination". For the Stoics, temperance is a vital part of navigating life's many choices and helping you decide what to embrace and what to avoid, especially in the face of constant temptations. As Seneca put it, "If a person doesn't know to which port they sail, no wind is favourable." If your destination is a life of happiness and fulfilment, you need self-discipline to sail through the inevitable temptations and obstacles that will arise.

Instead of trying to suppress desires, you can change your perspective on the things you avoid. For example, if you view exercise as a tedious chore, you can reframe it as a precious opportunity for personal contemplation, clearing your mind or as a means of revitalization. Mental shifts like this can help you embrace beneficial activities that you might otherwise dread.

You can also structure your life to minimize situations requiring self-control. For instance, if unhealthy snacks are a weakness, the wise choice is to refrain from buying them when you're at the grocery store. By doing so, you eliminate the temptation altogether, making it easier to adhere to your self-discipline and maintain your commitment to virtuous choices.

Read to challenge

Seneca wrote that "no man was ever wise by chance" – wisdom takes work and dedication. While acting virtuously is of course a vital part of Stoicism as a practical philosophy, it's also important to challenge your ideas. Epictetus said, "Books are the training weights of the mind" and they should be used to improve your thinking and to help you become "a more discriminating and reflective person". Read, listen to podcasts and challenge your own beliefs regularly, and be excited about what you are reading – read works that *you* enjoy and that resonate with you personally.

Every time I read a great book I felt I was reading a kind of map, a treasure map, and the treasure I was being directed to was in actual fact myself.

Matt Haig

Your natural goodness

Marcus Aurelius believed that performing good deeds is what nature requires of us. He wrote: "We ought to do good to others as simply as a horse runs, or a bee makes honey, or a vine bears grapes season after season without thinking of the grapes it has borne." Animals and plants carry out their functions without conscious calculation; humans should act with a similar sense of spontaneity and goodness. Make acts of kindness and virtue a fundamental part of your character, without seeking personal gain or acknowledgement. You could try helping an elderly neighbour with household chores, supporting local charities, regularly complimenting and encouraging others, or giving up your seat on public transport. Remember you have a duty as a human being to help others.

Modern life is flooded with information. It's why more and more people are seeking silence to quiet the noise in their ears and the chatter in their heads. But in that silence, many find something else stirs: an inner voice that leads to growth.

David DeSteno

Act with humility

Wavering between success and failure is a necessary part of life. Stoicism teaches us to be modest in our successes and to foster humility. Epictetus encouraged his students to recognize the limits of their control and to "be content to be thought foolish and stupid". Embrace failures as valuable lessons that contribute to personal growth, admit when you don't know the answer, learn from those around you and never consider yourself superior to anyone else. Adopt a mindset that values continuous learning and acknowledges the impermanence of success. Actively support others in their endeavours by offering encouragement and celebrating their achievements. Recognize that shared success strengthens our collective human connections and expressing enthusiasm for others' accomplishments fosters a positive and supportive community.

Think lightly
of yourself
and deeply
of the world.

MIYAMOTO MUSASHI

THE
VIRTUE
OF
JUSTICE

The Stoics defined justice more broadly than the way it's commonly understood today. Rather than pertaining to legal systems or how society is organized, justice in Stoic terms refers to the morality behind our actions and the duty we have to our fellow human beings. You can think of it as wisdom in your social life, specifically in relation to your community and the people within it. This chapter shows you how to practise this virtue in your social interactions and explains why it's important to treat everyone with respect, fairness and dignity – regardless of a person's social status or political perspective.

The Golden Rule

The Golden Rule, sometimes called an "ethics of reciprocity", is the principle of treating others as you would want to be treated. Versions of this idea exist in different religions and stories as far back as 1850 BCE in Ancient Egypt.

For the Stoics, the Golden Rule serves as a practical way to apply the idea that our own well-being is intertwined with the well-being of the whole human community (see page 41). In consideration of our common rationality and shared humanity, treat others with fairness, empathy and respect, just as you would desire for yourself. In this way, you promote harmonious social interactions and a just, compassionate society.

Being kind to one person might not change the world but it sure will change that one person's world.

MO GAWDAT

A citizen of the universe

The Stoic concept of *oikeiōsis* (derived from the Greek word for house) is variously translated as "appropriation" or "familiarization", and suggests the importance of treating others like they're part of your family. It is founded on the shared rationality of the entire human race. You can think of *oikeiōsis* as a continuum, stretching from the instinctive self-preservation of the new-born infant to the other-regarding conduct that is equally natural in adults. It's a concept that can help you to recognize your social responsibilities and duties towards other human beings.

Oikeiōsis encourages you to extend your concern, care and empathy to others, recognizing them as part of the same broader human family. There are many ways you can apply it to your life. For instance, you can:

- Expand your circle of concern beyond your immediate family and friends to encompass a broader community. You could offer assistance to those in need (such as supporting an elderly neighbour or helping a colleague), engage in community projects or initiate social events in your local area.

- Treat strangers and acquaintances with the same respect and kindness you reserve for loved ones.

- Cultivate empathy and compassion for others. Understand that, like you, they too have desires, fears and aspirations.

To forget our membership and responsibilities in the social world and how that affects our life chances is to forget who we are.

Nancy Sherman

Be cooperative

Stoics believe humans are inherently social creatures, and that our natural state is one of cooperation and harmony. As Marcus Aurelius said, "We were born to work together like feet, hands, and eyes, like the two rows of teeth, upper and lower. To obstruct each other is unnatural." Harming or being unjust to others goes against our natural disposition – conflict or violence disrupts the natural order and leads to discord and injustice. Recognize your interconnectedness with others and your shared goals; be a team player, actively listen to understand the perspectives and emotions of others and engage in random acts of kindness to foster a sense of connection. Strive for a fair and equal society where people work together, like the body's parts, for the common good.

Lead by example

Justice is not only an individual pursuit but also a collective effort to create a fair and peaceful society. The Stoics recognize that people learn less from being told what to do and more from observing the actions of others. Epictetus said: "On no occasion call yourself a philosopher, and do not speak much among the uninstructed about theorems, but do that which follows from them." If you demonstrate fairness, integrity and ethical conduct in your actions and decisions, you serve as a role model for the people around you. For instance, being honest in all your interactions, approaching decisions impartially and contributing to social causes sets a positive example for those around you.

Our greatness has always come from people who expect nothing and take nothing for granted – folks who work hard for what they have, then reach back and help others after them.

Michelle Obama

Give to your community

Many people are engaged in online activism about things happening far away, which can lead to a sense of hopelessness or empathy fatigue. To avoid taking well-intentioned but ultimately fruitless action, the Stoics believe we should practise the virtue of justice within our immediate circles. Direct your energy to the areas in life where you *do* have control and can have a direct impact on the well-being of society. There are many ways to do this, including:

- **Environmental Stewardship** – taking action to protect the environment, such as picking up litter, participating in clean-up efforts or supporting sustainable practices. This preserves natural resources for future generations.

- **Mentoring** – mentoring young people or providing guidance to those in need can help them access opportunities, promoting fairness and social mobility.

- **Volunteering** – by donating your time and skills to a local charity or nonprofit organization, you can help people receive assistance and support in their time of need, promoting fairness and social equilibrium.

Contributing to your community exemplifies justice by creating a fairer, cooperative environment for all.

Forgiveness is freedom

In Stoic philosophy, justice entails treating others fairly, not seeking revenge and avoiding undue harshness. Seneca said, "All cruelty springs from weakness" and this includes cruelty towards those who wrong you. Seneca's book *De Clementia (Of Clemency,* also translated as *On Mercy)* used "clemency" to describe how the powerful should treat the powerless, particularly when the less powerful person is at fault. Stoics believe that holding on to negative feelings like anger, resentment and hatred is destructive to well-being. For example, holding grudges against people who have hurt you can result in an excessive or vindictive response. Instead, choose forgiveness to maintain your inner peace. Empathize with the other person's perspective and recognize their own struggles and challenges. Let go of the expectation of an apology; being forgiving is about *your* healing, not their acknowledgement.

Forgiveness is giving
up the hope that
the past could have
been any different.

OPRAH WINFREY

Active listening

The Greek biographer Diogenes Laertius wrote that Zeno said to a young person who was talking irrationally: "The reason why we have two ears and only one mouth is so we might listen more and talk less." Stoics emphasize considering the perspectives of others, even when they differ from your own.

Practise active listening to truly understand others' feelings, showing respect for their views. You can do this by giving the speaker your full attention, maintaining eye contact, avoiding interruptions, asking open-ended questions and using welcoming body language, such as facing the person and maintaining a relaxed posture. This not only deepens your connection with them but also helps you respond more empathetically.

The art of
conversation
lies in listening.

MALCOLM FORBES

Take responsibility

The Stoics advised against excessive complaining and shifting blame onto other people; they believed that both habits hindered personal growth and social harmony. Instead, they promoted taking accountability for your actions and seeking fairness in your interactions with others. To foster a sense of empathy and focus on the choices you have, you can try the following:

- Understand the motivations and circumstances of people – be curious towards others rather than judgemental.

- Think about how you can change negative situations that arise in your life – avoid complaining about them and be proactive instead.

As Epictetus said: "Small-minded people blame others. Average people blame themselves. The wise see all blame as foolishness."

The greatest tragedy
for any human being
is going through their
entire lives believing the
only perspective that
matters is their own.

Doug Baldwin

Express gratitude

For the Stoics, gratitude is a mindset and an active practice – you have to express your gratitude in tangible ways. When we express gratitude, we recognize the contributions and kindness of others, which aligns with the Stoic idea that we should understand our interdependence and treat others justly. Living virtuously also includes recognizing the virtue in others; expressing gratitude helps you to appreciate the kindness, help or support you receive. You can express gratitude in several ways, including:

- Writing thank you notes for people who have helped you in any way.

- Saying "thank you" often, even for small actions.

- Taking regular walks in nature to appreciate the world around you.

- Avoiding people who often complain or are negative.

- Writing down three things you are grateful for every day (a gratitude journal may help with this).

Gratitude is a practical expression of justice because it encourages you to treat others fairly and recognize their virtues, and promotes a sense of interconnectedness. It also reduces feelings of discontent, envy and entitlement. As Epicurus wisely put it: "Remember that what you now have was once among the things you only hoped for."

To be a good human being is to have a kind of openness to the world, an ability to trust uncertain things beyond your own control.

Martha Nussbaum

Have realistic expectations

In one of Marcus Aurelius' most famous passages, he wrote, "Begin each day by telling yourself: today I shall be meeting with interference, ingratitude, insolence, disloyalty, ill-will, and selfishness." Human behaviour often fell short of expectations 1800 years ago, just as it does today, and emperors, like you, regularly encountered people behaving thoughtlessly. Marcus reminds us not to be surprised by this – you should always *expect* to encounter disappointing behaviour. If it comes as a surprise, it can trigger negative feelings and cause us to act irrationally. By being prepared every morning for the fact that people are flawed, you can control how you respond when foolish behaviour inevitably happens.

Identify what's important

In the twenty-first century, constant access to world events and others' personal lives can be overwhelming. Today, the average person consumes as much information in one day as a highly educated person read in their whole lifetime 500 years ago.

While technology was different in the time of the ancient Stoics, the temptation to procrastinate was the same. Marcus Aurelius wrote: "The attention you give to any action should be in due proportion to its worth." To avoid frittering life away, the Stoics urge you to always ask yourself, "Is this necessary?" Your time is limited and should not be wasted by mindlessly scrolling through social media, binge-watching irrelevant content or engaging in unproductive gossip; focus your words and energy on essential and enriching tasks.

In certain moments
when our minds and
hearts are not defended,
we experience love,
order, sense, beauty,
justice and all the other
ineffable good stuff.

Sharon Lebell

Don't underestimate people

Stoicism encourages us to approach people with an open mind, recognizing that each person has the potential to contribute to our shared understanding of life's fundamental principles. It teaches us to see the inherent value in every individual, recognizing that wisdom, virtue and strength of character can be found in the most unexpected places. This perspective is well illustrated in the history of Stoicism itself. The first three leaders of the Stoic school, Zeno, Cleanthes and Chrysippus, were immigrants who arrived in Athens with virtually no money.

They didn't fit the traditional profile of influential figures, yet their contributions to Stoic philosophy were immeasurable. Their stories exemplify the principle that wisdom and virtue are not bound by superficial factors like social status, wealth or origin.

You can embrace the Stoic virtue of justice by not underestimating the people you encounter. In the workplace, treat your colleagues and subordinates with fairness and respect, regardless of their job titles or backgrounds. Don't prejudge people based on their past mistakes or differences in opinion; offer second chances when appropriate and practise forgiveness. By recognizing the potential and value in every individual, you promote a more just and harmonious world.

If I had to summarize
all the scientific literature
on the causes of human
happiness in one word,
that word would be "social"
[...] your friends and family
and the strength of your
bonds with them.

Daniel Gilbert

Let virtue lead the way

Summum bonum, a central idea in Stoicism, refers to "the highest good" or ultimate goal that individuals should strive for in life. In practical terms, this means living a life in accordance with virtue and reason, prioritizing moral excellence and wisdom over external goods like wealth or fame. To apply this concept daily, practise self-reflection to ensure your choices align with the cardinal virtues of wisdom, courage, temperance and justice. Prioritize meaningful connections and the welfare of others over money and material possessions. Instead of pursuing transient, external rewards, focus your life on ethical principles and improving your character. Marcus Aurelius summarized this idea as: "Just that you do the right thing. The rest doesn't matter."

Challenge injustice

Throughout history, Stoics have demonstrated a commitment to creating a more just world. Marcus Aurelius described justice as "the source of all the other virtues". Contrary to the misconception that Stoicism promotes indifference, Stoics do not passively accept injustice; they courageously confront it by using the means at their disposal. This is a testament to their unwavering dedication to do the right thing.

During his 27 years of imprisonment, Nelson Mandela read *Meditations*. After his release, Mandela embodied Stoic principles in his leadership and reconciliation efforts in post-apartheid South Africa.

In 2019, following the massacre of 50 Muslims by one gunman in Christchurch, New Zealand, Prime Minister Jacinda Ardern travelled to the area affected and wore a hijab to display her respect, declaring, "Speak the names of those who were lost rather than the name of the man who took them. He may have sought notoriety but we in New Zealand will give him nothing – not even his name."

You don't have to be a world leader to actively challenge injustice – in your everyday life, you can speak out against discrimination, support sustainable practices, ensure fair treatment in your workplace and address disputes calmly. The outcome is not the focus; what matters is that you do your best to create a more peaceful and virtuous society.

A day in the life of a Stoic

Now that you've learned all about embracing Stoic values in order to live life as your best self, here's an example of how your day might look as a modern Stoic:

First light (5-7 a.m.)

Begin the day contemplating Stoic principles and affirming personal values.

Mindful morning routine (7-9 a.m.)

Focus on each task with full awareness and purpose. Do some moderate exercise, like a brisk walk or jog. Reflect on the beauty of the natural world.

Prioritize virtues (9 a.m.-6 p.m.)

As the day unfolds, engage in work with a focus on excellence and allocate a specific time for volunteering activities. Take a break at midday to spend time outdoors. Navigate challenges with resilience, adapting to what can be controlled and accepting the rest. Recognize the impermanence of external events and practise gratitude for experiences and relationships.

Evening reflection (6-7 p.m.)

Spend time in nature and reflect on your actions, decisions and contribution to social well-being. Identify areas for personal growth.

Social connections (7-9 p.m.)

Foster meaningful connections by practising empathy and understanding.

Cultivate inner peace (9 p.m. onwards)

Engage in practices that promote inner peace, such as stargazing, meditation and journalling, to conclude the day with mindfulness.

Reserve weekends for longer nature excursions (such as hiking) or any activity that allows for a deeper connection with the natural world. Designate a portion of every weekend for a digital detox.

Conclusion

Seneca wrote that "One has to accept life on the same terms as the public baths, or crowds, or travel. Things will get thrown at you and things will hit you. Life's no soft affair." Like the teachings of many Stoics, he acknowledges that, no matter who we are or where we come from, life is sure to be unpredictable and full of challenges.

For the Stoics, we are all equally foolish in the face of obstacles because only "the Sage" (a hypothetical ideal) has learned perfect wisdom. But don't let this discourage you; accepting that you are imperfect and mortal is both humbling and inspiring.

For over 2,000 years, Stoicism has helped people from across the world identify the best use of their precious time and energy.

Developing a virtuous character is a lifelong process of development; every day you have the power to focus on what is in your control and to surrender what is not.

These ancient teachings not only strengthen your character, but also inspire you to engage with life's enigmas. Stoic philosophy offers a pathway to enhanced well-being by guiding you to explore your unique purpose and to foster a deep appreciation for the virtues of those who surround you. It reminds you to appreciate the wonder of existence and the transformative force of gratitude.

No matter what life throws at you, Stoicism helps you capture the beauty amid the chaos and provides a guiding hand towards a life well-lived.

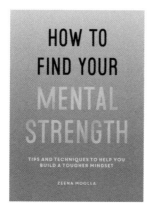

How to Find Your Mental Strength

Zeena Moolla

978-1-80007-187-2

Turn adversity into strength

In this book you will learn the benefits of cultivating a growth mindset, how you can harness the power of positive thinking, and tips and techniques for building your mental strength.

Learn how to manage everything from daily difficulties to life's unexpected challenges with this practical guide for a stronger, healthier you.

Life is Tough, But So Are You

Debbi Marco
978-1-80007-155-1

You can totally do this

We all face ups and downs from time to time, and if you sometimes struggle to cope with life's challenges, big or small, then this book can help. Bursting with useful tips, kind advice and encouraging affirmations, this handy guide will provide the tools you need to overcome adversity and bounce back even stronger.

This is the perfect book for anyone looking to find strength, survive setbacks, and foster a brilliant, more resilient mindset.

Have you enjoyed this book?

If so, find us on Facebook at
Summersdale Publishers,
on Twitter/X at **@Summersdale**
and on Instagram and TikTok at
@summersdalebooks and get in touch.

We'd love to hear from you!

www.summersdale.com